Tom Brassington & Joe Brassington

A picture book to help children share their feelings

unbound

First published in 2022

Unbound
Level 1, Devonshire House, One Mayfair Place, London W1J 8AJ
www.unbound.com
All rights reserved

Text design by PDQ Digital Media Solutions Ltd.

A CIP record for this book is available from the British Library

ISBN 978-1-80018-105-2 (hardback)
ISBN 978-1-80018-106-9 (ebook)

Printed in Slovenia by DZS

1 3 5 7 9 8 6 4 2

Bottled was built by a community – a community of people who see the value in emotional authenticity, who recognise the importance of talking about how you feel, and who have bravely shared your experiences of mental health and mental ill-health. This book is as much yours as it is ours.

It's our sincere hope that this book goes some way to helping others feel able to share their stories and create emotionally honest spaces in their lives.

Thank you to our supporters, friends and family.

This book is dedicated to Ellie, our sister. The bravest and most beautiful heart we know. Were it not for you, this book wouldn't exist. You're the best of our family, and we are infinitely better people because of you. Thank you.

With special thanks to the following patrons for their generous support:

Simon Atkinson
Andrew and Mandy Brassington
Bright Leaders
John Byrne
Sara Cliff
Ian Hunt
Phillip and Natasha Ingham
Colin and Kim Mitchell
Ilias Mitropoulos
The Parish Family
Onijali Rauf
Owen Romble
Jean Shilton
Kyrstie Stubbs
Ben Woolmer

David L Ball, in memory of Alison Ball

Ian and Jacquelyn Young, in memory of our beautiful son Matthew Thomas Young

This is a bottle.

You will have seen bottles before.

There are bottles that hold water,
bottles that hold lotions,
bottles that hold milk
and bottles holding potions.

But...

have you ever seen bottles
that hold...

...emotions?

Our world is a strange place
and many people try to claim
there are more differences between us
than things which are the same.

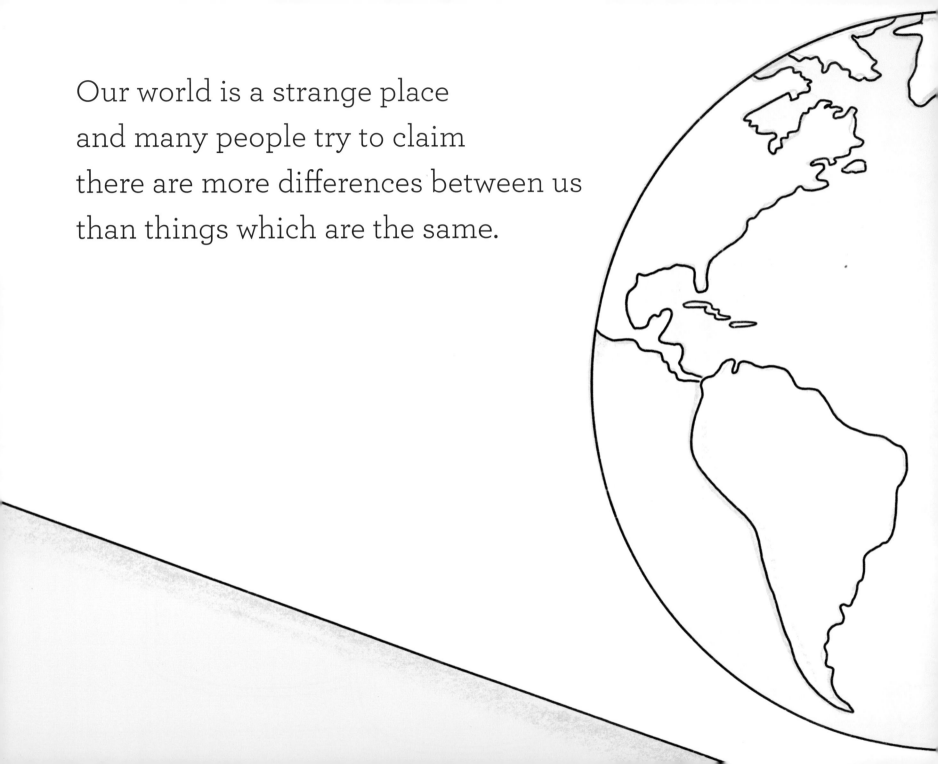

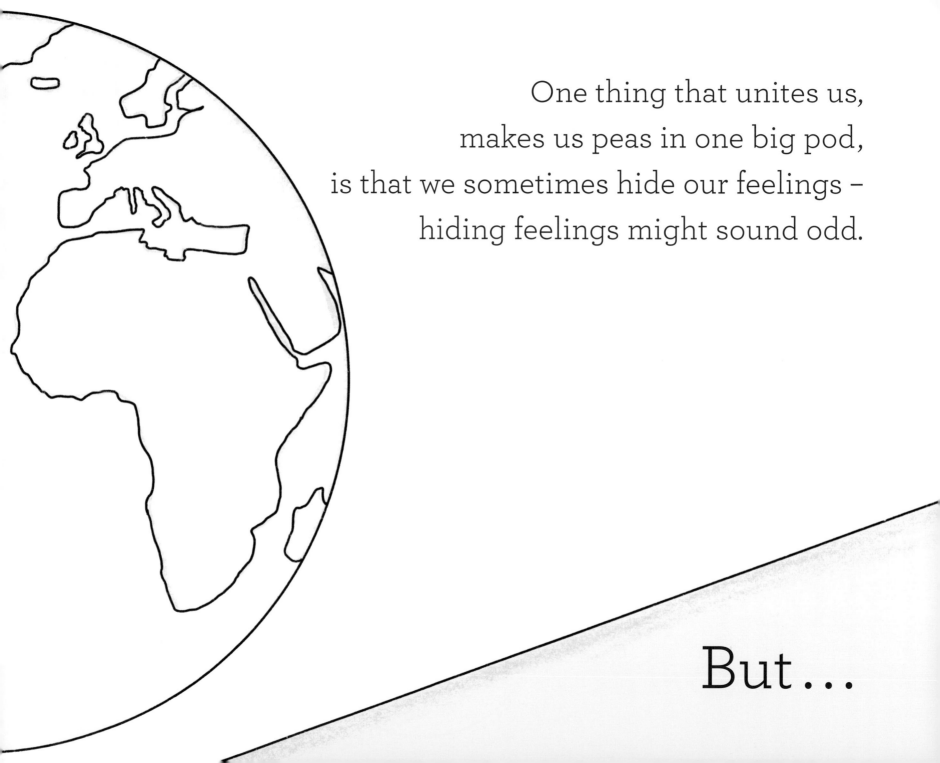

One thing that unites us,
makes us peas in one big pod,
is that we sometimes hide our feelings –
hiding feelings might sound odd.

But…

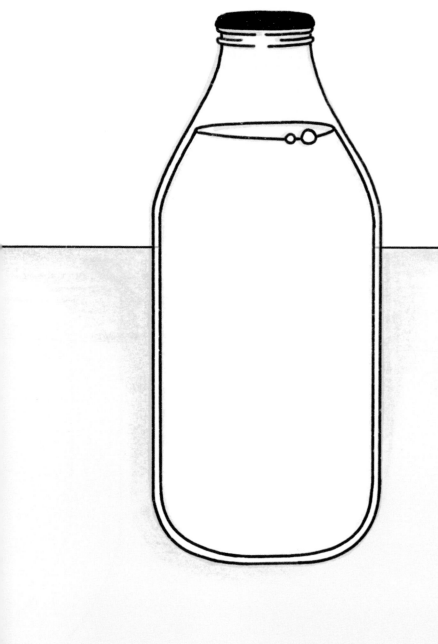

Other times we bottle them up, not ready to let them out.

We might bottle because it scares us.
We might pretend our feelings aren't there.
We might worry what others think
but act like we don't care.

We might think it's best to bottle
after trying to share before.
If people were unkind that time,
we might not share any more.

We might not want to bottle things up,
rather share how we're feeling now.
Maybe we don't have the words
because nobody taught us how.

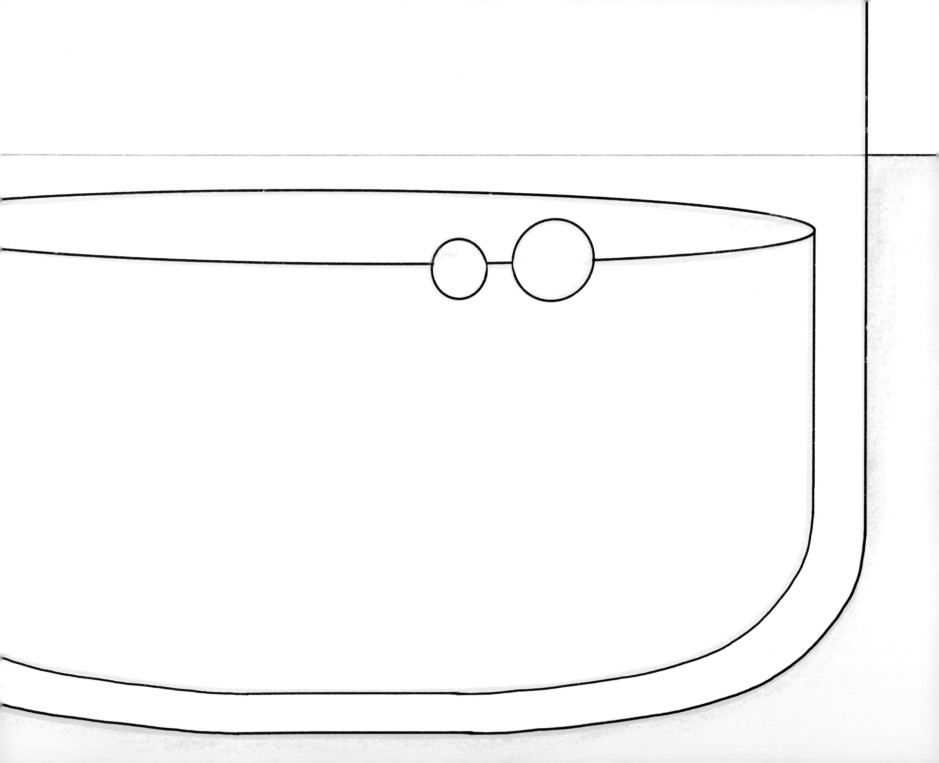

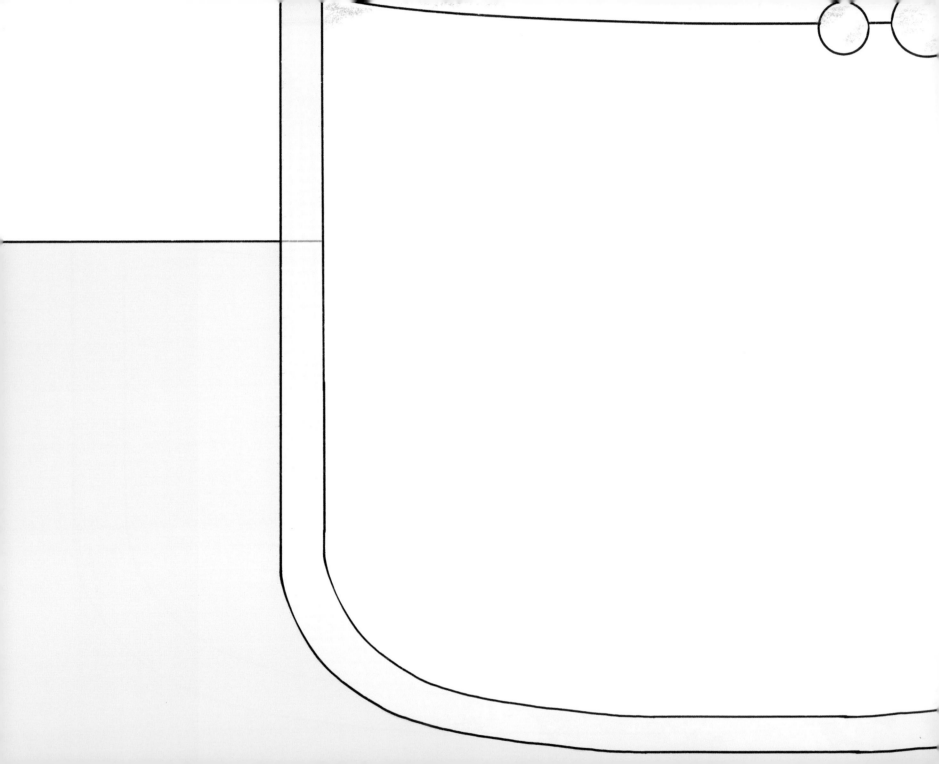

Even with our feelings bottled,
nestled deep inside,
it's hard to just ignore them –
they never *truly* hide.

Our bottles keep on filling up,
not knowing when to stop.
Each day, they just get heavier
till they're filled right to the top.

All bottles have their limits.
Have you ever tried,
to fill one up until it's full?
It can't all stay inside.

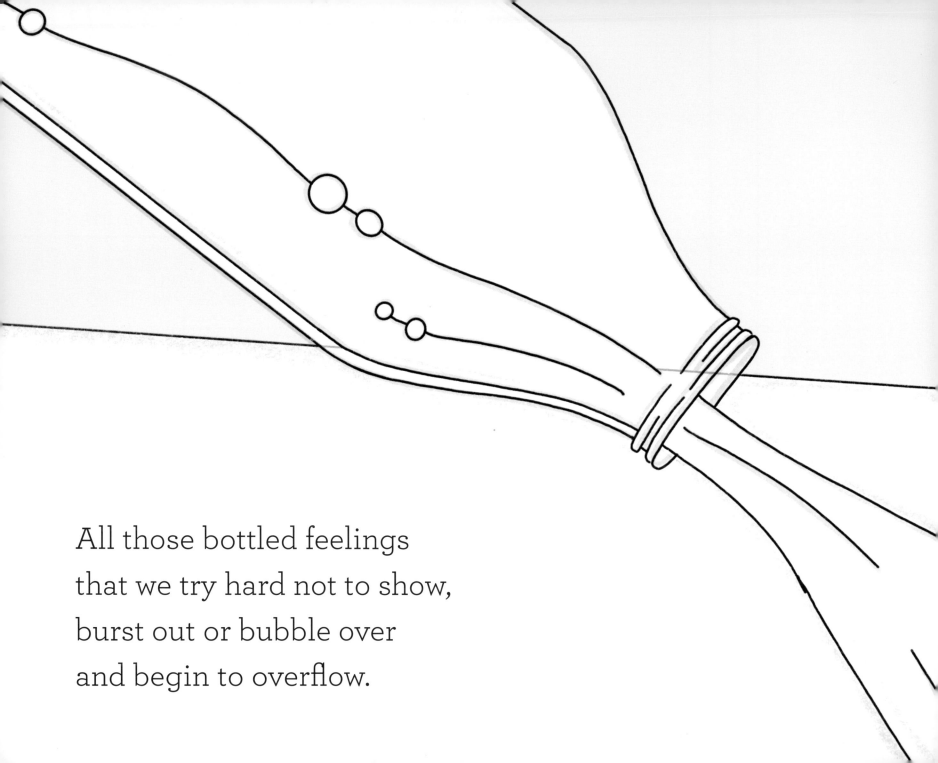

All those bottled feelings
that we try hard not to show,
burst out or bubble over
and begin to overflow.

Sometimes it feels so small –
a single tear in our eye.
Other times it feels so big
we cry and cry and cry.

Our bottles can get heavy;
our strength feels like it's gone.
If we have to keep on carrying,
we feel we can't keep carrying on.

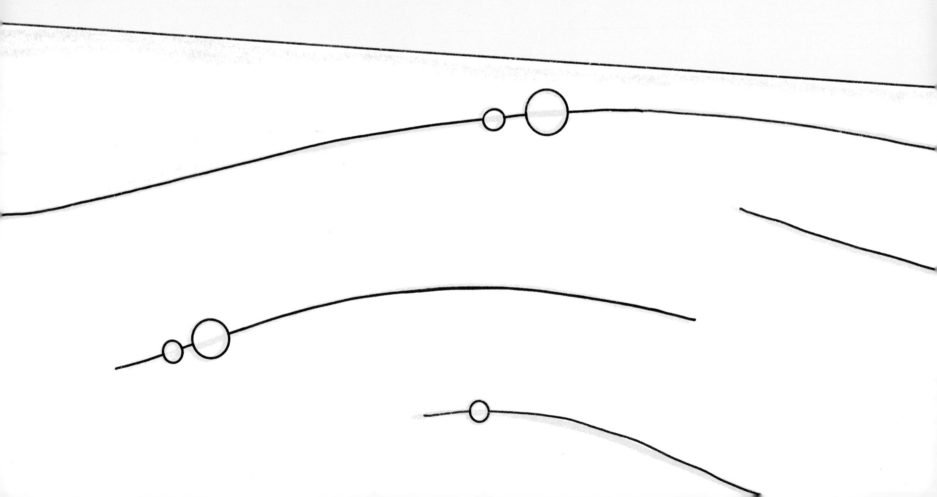

With a bottle that's too heavy
and strength that's not so strong,
it's easier to let things slip
and before very long…

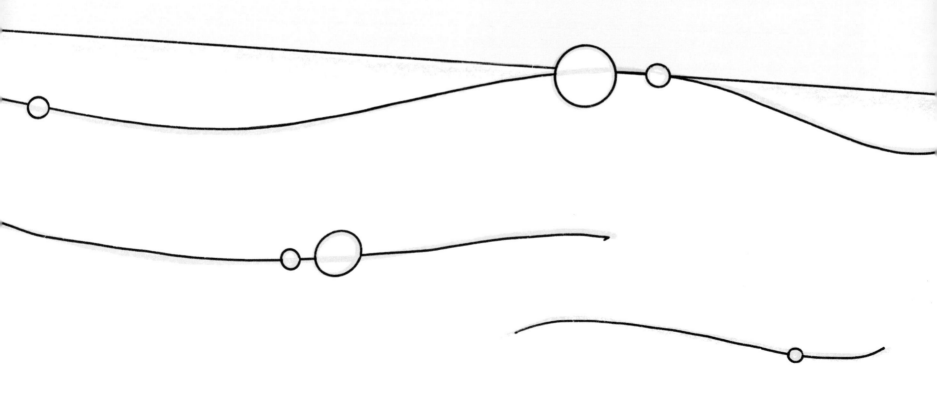

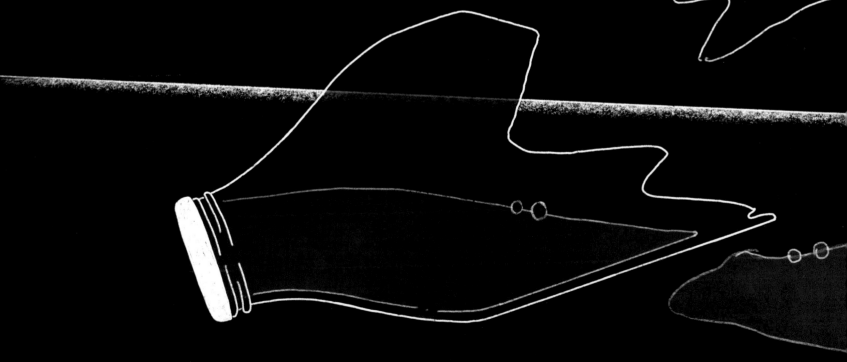

SMASH!

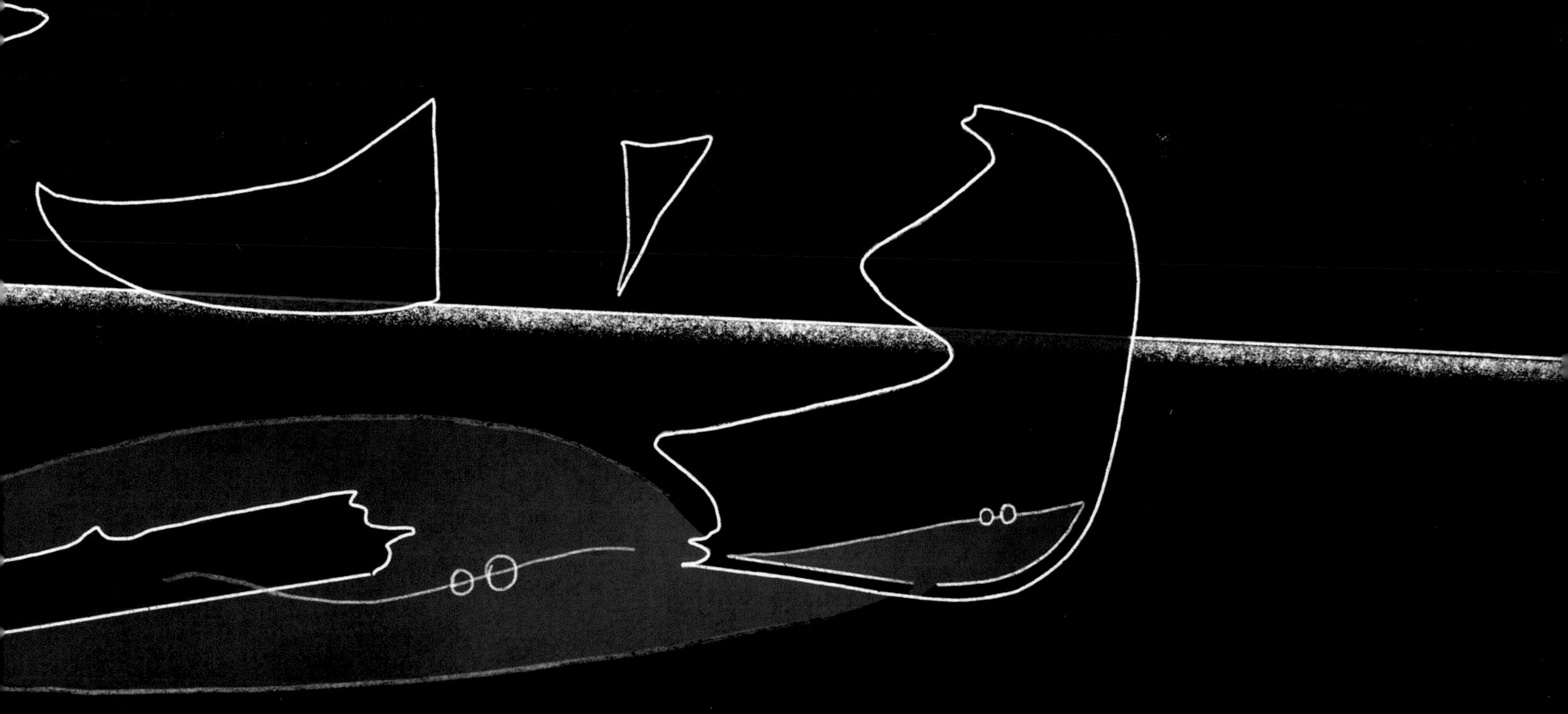

It can feel so very lonely.
Do people even care?
But how can someone help us
unless we start to share?

Sometimes it's good to keep things
bottled – we don't have to share it *all*.
But if we hold everything inside,
heavier bottles just might fall.

However...

…if we share how we're feeling,
if we talk to a trusted friend,
if we pour out what was bottled,
if we're honest and don't pretend,

carrying bottles becomes less daunting,
things feel a little bit lighter.
When we share how we are feeling,
our world starts to look brighter.

So when a friend, someone you trust,
asks, 'Hey, how are you?'
be brave
and be honest –
share the truth inside of you.

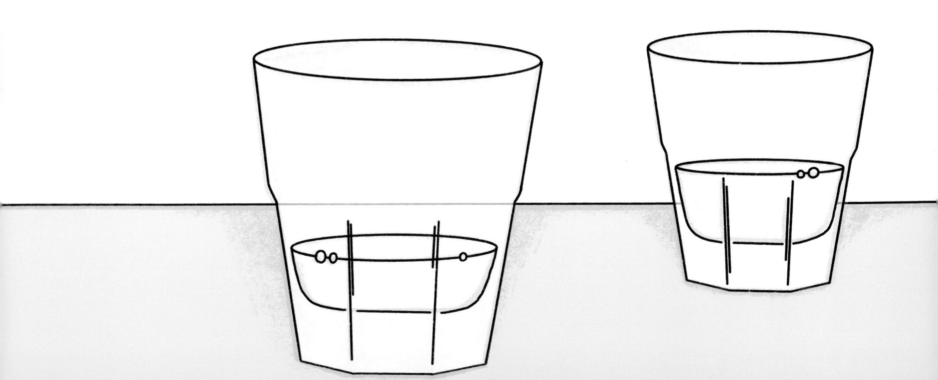

Then when you've finished sharing
and you've told them what is true,
reach out
and ask them back –
maybe they need to share too.

This is a bottle.

You will have seen bottles before.

What are you bottling up?
Maybe now's the time to explore.

Unbound is the world's first crowdfunding publisher, established in 2011.

We believe that wonderful things can happen when you clear a path for people who share a passion. That's why we've built a platform that brings together readers and authors to crowdfund books they believe in – and give fresh ideas that don't fit the traditional mould the chance they deserve.

This book is in your hands because readers made it possible. Everyone who pledged their support is listed below. Join them by visiting unbound.com and supporting a book today.

R. Gotts, Mateusz Grabski, Daniel Gray, Great Heath Primary Academy, Academy Transformation Trust, Emily Green, Jasmine Green, Rebecca Green, Ryan Green, Sean Green, Ms Greene and St Michael's Junior Church School , Georgia Greer, Sue Gregory, Ann Grendon, Angela Griffiths, Annabelle Griffiths, Lucy Griffiths, Tom Griffiths, Tamsin Grimmer, B Guerriero, Tim & Philippa Gunn, Helen Gunshon, Gemma Haley, Ian Hall, Phoebe Halliday, Karen Hambleton, Elizabeth Hamilton-Pearce, Ben Hancox, Laura Hands, Frank Hannigan, Jacob Hanson, Bekka Harcombe, Millie Hardy, Matthew Harker, Kirsty Harley, Louise Harling, Vikki Harper, Maria Harrington, David Harris, Helen Harrison, Katherine Harrison, Lindsey Harrison, Karen Hart, Jacqualine Hartle, Sara Hartshorn, Victoria Harvey, Daniel Hawkins, Noah Evelyn Alvina Hawley, Tanya Hawthorne, Gavin Hayes, Hannah Hayes, Laura Haynes, Jonny Heald, Louise Heard, Lyndsey Heard, Jonathan Heath, Vicki Heath, Martin Heeley, Becky Hendry, Philip Hewitt, Susan Higgins, Amy Hill, Betsan and Stephen Hill, Emma Hill, Gareth Hill, Kate Hill, Kerry Hill, Rhiannon Hill, Hillside High School , Jan Hobbis, Chris Hodgson, Lucy Hogg, Gemma Holden, Jane Hollywood, Alison Holtham, Jayne Hopkins, Tim Hopkins, Nicola Horobin, Mark Horsfall, Annalieza Horton, Macauley Horton, Tracy Hoskins, Libby Hough, Jade Howard, Charlotte Howarth, Amanda Howlett, Neil Hubbard, Melissa Hudson, Bekah Hughes, Kirsty Hughes, Vicki Hughes, Jo Hull, Richard Human, Sarah Hunter, Dr Jahan Hussain, Lyndsey Hyndman, Iceni Primary Academy, Academy Transformation Trust, In memory of Emily Clark, Remission Possible, Natasha Ingham, Joanne Ireland, Laura Ireland, Adam Jackson, Beth Jackson, Harley Jackson, Joseph and Adam Jackson, Theo James, Amanda Jarrett, Christine Jenkins, Laura-Jayne Johnson, Victoria Johnson, Lacey Joinson, Briony Jones, James Jones, Jessica Jones, Mark Jones, Natalie Jones, Jubilee Primary Academy, Academy Transformation Trust, Maria Justice, Jamie Kavanagh, Laura Kayes, Danielle Keen, Helen Kelly, Sorcha Kelly, Jen Kenny, Rachel Kenny, Jeanette Khan, Henry Kiddy, Dan Kieran, Steph Kimble, The King Family, Kingsmoor Primary Academy, Academy Transformation Trust, Nikola Kinmond-Jones, Rosanna Kinsella, Amy Knight, Ellie Knott, Judith & Jonathan Knott, Chris Konrath, Katarzyna Krawczyk, Mal Krishnasamy, Charlie Lambert, Keith Lamley, Bryony Landsbert, Polly Langford, Benji Lanky, Mrs Rachel Laud, Hannah Lavin, Michelle Law, Lyn Lawrence, Jacqueline Lawton, Julie Le Feuvre, Anne Leatherland, Michelle Lee, Sarah Lee, Tracy Levitt, Jayne Lindsay, Andy Logan, Callum Logan, Nicola Lomas, Eliane Louden, Skye LoVecchio, Lucy , Rebecca Lucy, Cynthia Ludford-Brooks, Carrie Lumsden, Joe Luscombe, Chelsea Lynaugh, Hannah MacGregor, Edyta Machczynska, Sam Mackey, Marija Maher Diffenthal, Tracy Main, Kathryn Marsh, Abi Martin, Joanna Martin, Wes Mason, Lucy Massey, Eve Masters, Pani Matsangos, Rhian Matthews, Hannah Maxwell, Julie Maxwell, Phil McCahill, Rob McCann, Muire McCarthy, Ellen McCartney, Angela McCombe, Dominique McConnachie, George McCormack, Matthew McCrum, Emma McDonald, Shelley McIntosh, Chloe McKee, Brian Mcleish, Margare Mclennaghan, Sarah McLoughlin, Siobhan McManamon, James McMordie, Kira & Corey McNay, Sophie Mcvicar, Lily & Matthew Meade, Rob Meakin, Tertia Meakin, Annisa Mehmood, Emma Mercer, Sarah Merchant, Josh & Ben Meredith , Fiona Micklefield, Oliver Mills, Sally Mills, Rose Millward, Jenny Mingus, Lisa Minifie, Liberty Minoli, Kim Mitchell, John Mitchinson, Daisy & Alfie Mole, Kerry Moloney, Nina Monksfield, Andy Moor, Catherine Moore, Lucie Moore, Tracy Moore, Emma Morgan, Kirsty Morris, Helen Mortimer, Joshua Mosiuk, Christopher Moss, Sue Moss, Susan Mould, Andrew Moxon, Catherine Mulhern, Claire Mumford, Haley Muraleedharan, Sarah Murphy, Andy Murray, Claire Myers, Zara Nargis, Anita Nathan, Carlo Navato, Al, Danah & Maia Nazaruk, Louise Nevin, Wilfred Newson, Esther Nisbet, Donna Nolan, Karen North, Sheila North, North Walsall Primary Academy, Academy Transformation Trust, Lydia O'Callaghan, D O'Carroll, Sue O'Malley, Oakley & Maisie , Nadia Obrzut, Fiona Okai, Joe Franklin Alice Oldfield, John OLeary, Tyson Oliver, Elisha Owen, Ethan Owen, Nicola Owen, Andrea Ozzy, Kim Padmore, Michelle Page, Josh Paling, Kathryn Palmer, Lisa Palmer, Parents Hub Derby, Anthony Parker, Harriet Parker, Lauren Paskin, Mary Passmore, Michelle Pate, Lizzie Pattison, Lynne Pattison, Nick Pattison, Kim Peacock, Emily Peake, Thomas Pearce, Mandy Pearson, Russell Pearson, Sarah Pearson, Lisa Pegg, Lucy Pendleton, Victoria Pendry, Chris Penglase, Jon, Abigail, and Amos Pepler, Lorna Perkins, Charles Perry, Dan Peters, Abigail Petherbridge, M Petticrew, Phoenix Academy, Academy Transformation Trust , Melanie Pickford, Jonathan Pilgrim, Emanuela Pingiori, Hazel Pinner, Ian Plenderleith, Justin Pollard, Gabriel Polski, Jojo & Dougie Potts, Adele Pratt, Max Preston, Alexia Pudney, Zara Pudney, Caroline Pulver, Daniel Pye, Gary Pykitt, Sarah Quiatt, Dermot Quinn, Sarah Quinn, Jennifer Rackham, Joanna Raczka, Ravens Primary Academy, Academy Transformation Trust, Susie Ray, Felicity Record, John & Rachel Redeemed, Claire Reed, Laura Reid, Susan Reid, Remembering Calum Downes , Rachel Renshaw, Abby Restall, Joanna Reynolds, Rhiannon & Charlie, Rachel Rhodes, Florry Rich, Ali Richardson, Michele Riley, Kerry Rini, Louisa Ritchie, Mrs Robayna, Daniel Robb, Leigh Roberts, Lyndsey Roberts, Tony Roberts, Ellice Robertson, Louis Robertson, Jenya Robinson, Nick Robinson, Sam Robson, Sarah Rodriguez, Katy Roelich, Louisa Nicole Rose, Jessica Rose Cambridge, Andrew Ross, Rosie Ross, Nichola Rossall, Emily Rought-Brooks, Charlotte Rowden, Helen Rowland, Melanie Rowland, Kristina Royle, Maria Rupp, Sigrid Rutishauser-James, A S, Lucy Salmon, Steven Salmon, Carol Salt, Allie Sanderson, Koren Sanderson, Dawn Sandiford, Kim Sands, Paul Sands, Amy Sattin, Kate Sawyer, Sue Saxon, Samantha Schmidt, Laura Scott, Anna Seely, Ceri Seymour, Lauren Sharpe, Helen Sheen, Fallon Sheffield, Terry Shenton, Reuben Sherratt, Claire Shipp, Sarah Siggs, Alison Simpkins, Stephen Simpson, Rich Simpson, Sam Sims, Beth Slater, Sarah Slattery, Beth Sleet, Sarah Small, Alice Smith, Amy Smith, Claire Smith, Clare Smith, Emma Smith, Jane Smith, Kay Smith, Lauren Smith, Leslie Smith, Nikki Smith, Philip Smith, Sarah Smith, Simon Smith, Annabel Smout, Laura Solley, Patricia Somerset, Ann Spencer, Deborah Spiers, Helen Spokes, St Modwen's Catholic Primary School, St Stephen's

Tom Brassington and Jo Brassington are brothers and both primary school teachers living and working in England. They are passionate about facilitating open and honest conversations about mental well-being in education, and creating emotionally honest spaces.

@BottledBook
www.anemotionallyhonestspace.co.uk